Contents

Our Oceans

Water covers most of planet Earth. A lot of animals live in different parts of the oceans, from scary sharks to wobbly sea jellies and giant whales.

In danger

The oceans are in trouble. Find out what is harming them and the animals that live in them, and what you can do to help.

Save the OCEANS

Sarah Levete

Crabtree Publishing Company

www.crabtreebooks.com

Author: Sarah Levete
Editors: Kathy Middleton
Crystal Sikkens
Project coordinator: Kathy Middleton
Production coordinator: Ken Wright
Prepress technicians: Ken Wright
Margaret Amy Salter

Picture Credits:
Corbis: Martin Harvey: page 14
Dreamstime: Carmina Jinga: page 20; Miehmann78:
page 12; Olga Sapegina: page 9; Tim Heusinger
Von Waldegge: page 21
Melbourne Zoo: page 11
Shutterstock: cover, Ilya Andriyanov: page 15; Rich
Carey: page 4; Cbpix: page 5; EcoPrint: page 6;
Marcus Efler: page 18; EpicStock: page 8;
Ivanova Inga: page 7; Tyler Olson: page 10;
Pborowka: page 16; Tonobalageurf: page 13;
Tubuceo: page 17; Jan Martin Will: page 19

Every effort has been made to trace copyright holders and to obtain their
permission for use of copyright material. The authors and publishers
would be pleased to rectify any error or omission in future editions.
All the Internet addresses given in this book were correct at the time of
going to press. The author and publishers regret any inconvenience
caused if addresses have changed or sites have ceased to exist, but can
accept no responsibility for any such changes.

Library and Archives Canada Cataloguing in Publication

Levete, Sarah
Save the oceans / Sarah Levete.

(Crabtree connections)
Includes index.
ISBN 978-0-7787-7857-8 (bound).--ISBN 978-0-7787-7879-0 (pbk.)

1. Marine pollution--Juvenile literature. 2. Marine ecology--
Juvenile literature. 3. Marine animals--Juvenile literature.
I. Title. II. Series: Crabtree connections

GC1090.L495 2011   j577.7'27   C2011-900604-9

Library of Congress Cataloging-in-Publication Data

Levete, Sarah.
Save the oceans / Sarah Levete.
p. cm. -- (Crabtree connections)
Includes index.
ISBN 978-0-7787-7879-0 (pbk. : alk. paper) --
ISBN 978-0-7787-7857-8 (reinforced library binding : alk. paper)
1. Ocean--Juvenile literature. 2. Marine pollution--Juvenile
literature. I. Title.
GC21.5.L48 2011
577.7'27--dc22

2011001341

Crabtree Publishing Company

www.crabtreebooks.com   1-800-387-7650

Printed in the U.S.A./072011/WO20110114

Published in Canada
Crabtree Publishing
616 Welland Ave.
St. Catharines, Ontario
L2M 5V6

Published in the United States
Crabtree Publishing
PMB 59051
350 Fifth Avenue, 59th Floor
New York, New York 10118

Our oceans

Clownfish live in warm oceans around the world. An **ocean** is a large area of salty water.

My home

Turtles live in oceans.

Oceans Alive

Ocean animals and plants live in different parts of oceans. Some live in shallow seawater near the shore, others in deep water far out at sea.

Along the shore

Look for some shallow swimmers:

1. Scoop up some seawater with a bucket.
2. Look to see which animals you have caught. Don't forget to put them back!

In the deep

Some cuttlefish live in the deep parts of oceans. They squirt ink at animals that try to eat them.

Hey!

Some crabs live in shallow water.

Dirty Water

Much of the **waste** we pour down our sinks ends up in the oceans. This waste is harmful to many animals and can **poison** them.

Cleaning up

Help keep oceans clean:

1. Don't pour **oil** or oily paint down the sink.
2. Take oily waste to the recycling center.

Keep it clean!

Poisoned!

Dirty seawater can kill animals, such as this dolphin.

surfer

Who wants to surf in dirty water?

9

Dumped

Some people use the oceans as a dump. They think garbage just sinks to the bottom of the sea. Wrong!

In the garbage can, not on the beach

Help keep beaches clean:

1. Don't leave garbage on the beach.
2. Don't drop litter in the street. Rain can wash it down the sewers and into the oceans.

Don't litter!

plastic

Garbage kills

Some ocean animals try to eat garbage, such as plastic. This can kill them.

Litter on the beach floats out to sea.

11

Something's Fishy

Fish are tasty to eat and good for us, but how we catch them can harm other animals that live in the oceans.

Good fishing

Catch fish without harming the oceans:

1. Don't catch too many fish.
2. Make sure other animals are not trapped in fishing nets.

fishing boat

line

Just a few

People who fish with a fishing pole don't catch too many fish. They take only the fish they need.

Too much!

Too many big fishing boats catch too many fish.

Dirty Oil

We get some of our oil from the seabed. It is sent along pipes to ships, but sometimes the pipes leak. The leaked oil sticks to ocean animals.

Helping animals

To clean a seabird safely:

1. Ask an **expert** to wash the bird.
2. Keep it safe until it is healthy.

Sticky and stuck

Birds covered in oil cannot move at all.

Sticky oil

Oil spreads into the ocean like thick, black syrup. It sticks to birds and ocean animals.

oil

Colorful Coral

Pink, yellow, and white **coral** are made up of tiny animals. Coral is beautiful, but it can break easily.

Looking after coral

Everyone can protect coral by:

1. Keeping oceans clean so coral can grow.
2. Keeping boats away from coral. They can smash it into pieces.

Save our home!

A lot of fish live on coral.

coral

Be careful

Divers like to look at coral, but they must be careful not to break pieces off.

Too Warm

Burning **coal** and oil makes **energy**, but it is making Earth warmer. This is bad news for ocean animals.

Cool down!

To help stop Earth warming up:

1. Save energy by turning off lights.
2. Take a shower, not a bath.
3. Recycle as much as possible.

Feeling the heat

seaweed

The oceans are getting too warm for some ocean animals.

sea ice

fish

Melting ice

The **sea ice** on which polar bears hunt for seals is melting faster in summer.

Safer Oceans

Speedboats race across water where ocean animals swim. If one hits an ocean animal, it can hurt or kill it.

Pass on the message

Tell everyone to help to save the oceans:

1. Make a "Save the Oceans" poster. Write on it all the things that people can do to help save the oceans.
2. Put the poster up in your school.

Stay away!

Slow down!
Many **manatees** have scars on their backs from crashes with speedboats.

scar

Speedboats hurt ocean animals if they hit them.

Glossary

coal Hard, black material that is burned for energy

coral Hard, often colorful, material made up of tiny ocean animals

divers People who use special equipment to swim beneath the sea

energy Power from burning coal and oil and other fuels. Machines use energy to work.

expert Person who knows a lot about something, or is very good at something

manatees Large sea mammals

ocean Large area of salty water

oil Thick, black liquid that is burned for energy

poison Harm or kill something

sea ice Seawater that has frozen

waste Garbage or things no longer wanted

Further Reading

Web Sites

Click on the coral reef overview to find out more about coral reefs at:
www.coral.org/resources/about_coral_reefs

WWF is an organization that tries to protect animals and the places in which they live. Find out more at:
wwf.panda.org/about_our_earth/blue_planet

You can find out a lot of information about the oceans at:
**http://school.discoveryeducation.com/
schooladventures/planetocean**

Books

Deep Sea Extremes by Natalie Hyde,
Crabtree Publishing (2009).

Animals of the Sea and Shore by Ann O. Squire,
Children's Press (2002).

Destroying the Oceans by Sarah Levete,
Crabtree Publishing (2010).

Index